the fissures of our throats

ESSENTIAL POETS SERIES 227

Canada Council **Conseil des Arts**
for the Arts **du Canada**

ONTARIO ARTS COUNCIL
CONSEIL DES ARTS DE L'ONTARIO

an Ontario government agency
un organisme du gouvernement de l'Ontario

Guernica Editions Inc. acknowledges the support of the Canada
Council for the Arts and the Ontario Arts Council. The Ontario Arts
Council is an agency of the Government of Ontario. We acknowl-
edge the financial support of the Government of Canada through
the Canada Book Fund (CBF) for our publishing activities.

the fissures
of our throats

Larry, with gratitude for your friendship
Edward
8/18/14

edward nixon

GUERNICA

TORONTO – BUFFALO – LANCASTER (U.K.)
2014

Michael Mirolla, editor
Elana Wolff, poetry editor
Guernica Editions Inc.
1569 Heritage Way, Oakville, ON L6M 2Z7
2250 Military Road, Tonawanda, N.Y. 14150-6000 U.S.A.

Book design by Jamie Kerry of Belle Étoile Studios
www.belleetoilestudios.com

Distributors:
University of Toronto Press Distribution,
5201 Dufferin Street, Toronto (ON), Canada M3H 5T8
Gazelle Book Services, White Cross Mills,
High Town, Lancaster LA1 4XS U.K.

First edition.
Printed in Canada.

Legal Deposit – Third Quarter
Library of Congress Catalog Card Number: 2104934821

Library and Archives Canada Cataloguing in Publication
Nixon, Edward A. E., 1960-, author
The fissures of our throats / Edward Nixon.
(Essential poets series ; 227)
Poems.
Issued in print and electronic formats.
ISBN 978-1-55071-993-2 (pbk.).
--ISBN 978-1-55071-994-9 (epub).
--ISBN 978-1-55071-995-6 (mobi)
I. Title. II. Series: Essential poets series ; 227
PS8627.I96F58 2014
C811'.6   C2014-900247-5   C2014-900248-3

Contents

*To my old west coast friends who believed, with love
and gratitude, Ken, Marni, Victoria, and Helen.*

*And to my "first" Toronto friends who have
walked with me through this or that: love and
gratitude, Allen, Janet, and Michael.*

To Anne Marie who said there would be a book.

at the edge of the dig

Possibly   (bone stylus)
Suggest   (cut tablet rhetoric)
Reason   (grunt task argument)
Evidence   (temple factory)
Poison   (salt soured ground)
Theory   (grainy rate of decay)
Scrap   (split proximal phalanx)
Postulate   (bath house frescos)
Rewrite   (sundial fractions)
Propose   (lyric submission)

proceed in an orderly fashion

After the soft things tore,
we learned to sew seaweed,
read clear-cut patterns from blown salt.

She recalled talk of zed and zee,
the blunt gentility of consonants
properly framed for closer reading.

Days spent far from burnt forests –
drinking solidarity from a fair-trade cup –
a causal fall from monochrome pain.

All could choose, if it were desired
to work with what was left.
Fractured uses – uncertain objects,

rendered from yesterday's constraints.
Smiles came easily,
experiment was bitter effort.

essay

Let there be a firmament in the midst of the waters,
and let it divide the waters from the waters.

He also brought of the firstlings of his flock,
then read on, dreaming systems of control.

If you love Jesus let tender fingers skip –
Cain loathing Abel's executive charm.

Jealousies combine in downtown Enoch –
Mrs. C says nothing makes her happy here.

At home Daddy shakes for Lilith as he
stitches costumes from twigs and lambskin.

Eve lights signal fires on her tongue –
exhales billows of charcoal prophecy.

Odd righteous men, some dodgy women,
water swallowing tongues. You could die here.

Lilly insists oxygen ruined much – garden-work
begat brassy humps, hookups authorized and not.

Lil lets Eve trace back to an original singe –
lick along her tender seam of knowing.

The girls agree legend should be better cast –
audition a desert lion, wild with holy doubt.

when we agreed

They watched buffalo run (we'll say)
for uncounted days into that country.

The wolves shaped sharp sticks.
Children were buried with flowers.

Snow stung eyes, as the tracking wind
threaded blood-sounds, sweet in the mouth.

Bones of monsters marked their borders.
We cut long lines to show we were human.

Moon campfires – astronauts constructed
a longhouse tuckpointed to darker stars.

When commuters first saw the mountains,
seeds stuck in their throats, word husks

littered the shoulders of the Yellowhead.
Big Horn leapt from tree line into clouds.

east of there

Lions lived outside,
we walked among them.
Some stayed
close enough to smell the rotting vines
and made their camp.
We moved further east,
not forgetting
the sense of us and us against force –
a longing for words to be
Sweet Scented Bedstraw
White Spruce
summer ice in the cedars.
The run of elk through moonwash.

we told stories as we ran

There was no particular that set things apart.
Ice vaporized when subjected to heat,
peaches would resist when unripe,

sarcasm worked more or less with most.
The main thing, if it can be said there was,
and it cannot be or could not then have been,

as it was not yet in our eyes like the dawn star,
when she appears proximate the moon,
or like why birds talk to the night:

meanings were not simply to be given easy.
And that was maybe like the new,
staining us with haphazard wanting.

We could have strained together, but
wonder was reserved as we deciphered,
tossed it around, argued bone, sang stone.

It came that we understood repetitive marks,
which was handy for the next part;
though some furrowed with objective worry.

You could have formed factions, but why?
We had been given the scouring wind.
When it was retold, most nodded with ease.

No one saw it all together, or mashed in one –
leaves crushed under bitter rock to make tea.
The young took time to make a theory here,

or stare at parts of the sky on a dare.
There was thought of claiming that or this,
but we'd walked from the receiving of names.

So the hunt was blood-breath in green distance,
our chatter – sound chasing after absent game.
On the plain we ran on with a dangerous joy.

summer of love

Merc 67. Fuel-burn conspicuous.
Burgundy speed box, fast on I-5.
Slow border morph to Highway 99.

Hey, hey, hey just got back from the USA.

Spared conifers, low-slung bungalows
sentinel the suburban slope.
Rhododendrons encroach the deck.

"Sunny Goodge Street" intersects Granville.
Tom Northcott. Summer's chart topper.
Vogue. Orpheum. Capitol.

Smashing into neon lights in their stillness.

Summer of Love, second grade.
Boys and girls of Wescott Elementary
learn their letters and measures:

Marijuana, LSD, Scientists make it.
Teachers take it. Why can't we?

Kerrisdale and Altamont cousins
dig narrative certainty, hunt
Easter eggs above the fog line.

The hip teens spin The Collectors,
turn on the British Properties.
Psychedelia sibilates the billiard room.

Look at a baby, what do you see?

I-Spied hippies on Third Beach.
Cut alphabets by the zigzag shore.
Called it play and let it be.

clinton at 45 below

Propane translates to sludge.
Breath contrails in the house.

Dad mixes up a diesel marinade,
scrap-wood necklacing
the grey-frosted tank:
duct-taped oven thermometer,
precarious ...
Now light the match son.
OK Dad!

OK Dad ...
My words cluster on the ice gravel.
Jimmy's father yaps
from the two-by-four portico
of his double-wide
as my old man minds
flame-licks.
I stand ready to smother fire
with brittle snow.

august, lake

We sank stones to the shit-mud bottom.
Shawnigan grifts a wobble of pigments
from pine needles, sky, bark, granite,
the wharf's pewtered cedar planks.

Shawnigan's surface wobble grifts
Mount Baldy from the far shore
the wharf's creaking cedar planks,
familial syllables that tie the dock.

Mount Baldy on the far shore.
The near rock I swam to at thirteen.
Cousins' syllables on the dock,
urging adolescent bones to float.

The outcrop I swam past at thirteen.
I showed you once, Oregon Grape,
cracked bones sunk into ochre mud.
Salal clusters, a berry's indigo blood.

cariboo ghost town

We found the fall-down cabins
leant against a predicate.
The arrangement suggested a rough consensus,
fell in with circles and doors facing their agreement.
Now a village fraction in moss decline
quarter mile from the claim.

Gold was in the ground and much was said about it.
Reliable studies contest this scrap of turf:
A rusted-shovel Utopia?
An outpost of imperial commerce?

We see their piss-house ruin,
the wildflowered fire-pit.
grasses, tumbleweed, an alkaline pond,
milled and nailed wood in slow rot.

You write notes as I take in pictures,
argue footnotes the hour back to 100 Mile House.
At the motel room you exhale on the pillow
in a damp accent I can't recover.

free translation

Translating the world back to you –
Prince Valiant interleaved
with cottage kindling –
an old knight's wormy alphabet.

Beard-burdened, the solitary one
tramps the paths of exile.
The Lady, Melanie of Burnaby – lost,
her data cracklings roasted, spoilt.

Bone chips and beads make a nice curtain,
but you, scrivener, cannot spell –
the margins are run with throes.
In whose pages did you swim and drown?

The raw men of Duncan had other pleasures.
Héloïse reticulates apology on newsprint.
Monks marching to war (only last year),
late arrows repelled by Anglican Bibles.

A wanderer spittled with grief,
hunts the 2-D fens of 4-panel dreams.
Transits his sorrowful spirit-chest,
a rough hack parsing an old clear-cut.

The boy's own comic in ashes –
the one-eyed dog on golden wheels
guards the outer border of the fire fender.
How in youth he feasted on tenebrous air.

verandah

The tongue and groove
... chicken-wire screens,
the peeling X-beams
see-through to lapping water
... a simple star and its name
... blackening pines
returning arguments ...
a space immixed with other scraps.

Words cut in and out of the dusky foam
we spoke of on holidays:
... laughter from the lake mist ...
the vacuum tube rumble ...
Radio Vladivostok, Pacific
shortwave ...
as the moon sharpens ...

Like the way our talk went
from easy ears into synaptic
roundabouts
as we chatted up
a thing about letters, light –
the insistent "I" ...
got messed
around and passed
into a "we" ...
a kind multiple –
these under-words of ours ...

as dusk tugged us
toward this stuff
we sassed and sauced about,
chewing through a plug
of notions ...

as tea and bourbon were portioned out
… by the woman we loved …
our lexical trill lilting
from the fissures of our throats.

lacan at the ovaltine

Writings scatter to the winds
blank cheques in an insane charge.
  – Jacques Lacan

This smudged buzz of the sign,
her cranking into a familiar vein –

Seahorse neon focal at *The Only* –
oyster-bright Cold War kids,

possessed, in post-punk dress-up,
slurping chowder in a cool frame.

Overpass, the junkie's walk-on-by –
confetti snark at the U countertop.

Quoting Lacan at the Ovaltine,
keening tightly kerned positions –

lipstick on an *Army & Navy* mug –
hint of tin, wisp of lemon gasoline.

Surfing a homegrown noetic high,
Town Pump flâneurs bleed out

a shivered upchuck politics –
dogma as a skid-row diorama.

nights in the city of the dead

*What needs to be said at the beginning is that the
single most impressive aspect of the present time – at
least for the "humanist," a description for which I have
contradictory feelings of affection and revulsion – is
that it is manifestly the Age of Ronald Reagan.*
     – Edward Said

*Je vais vous dire un grand secret ...
N'attendez pas le Jugement dernier.
Il a lieu tous les jours.*
     – Albert Camus

*I'm getting pretty angry, and I want to get out. Man.
And it's no good to shout. I'm getting fucking pissed off
you know, and I'm tired of going downtown.*
     – The Demics

I

In this particular darkness
guess freedom ...
a shit-noun ...

dank air,
exposed skin,
a soft constraint.

If I resist
ice-marrow
in finger-bone –
overwrite the margin,

essay a slight shit-kick
to conditioning?

II

Osgoode Hall fog-smothered.
Spittle dew despoils
crisp rolling paper.
Match struck.
Night-leaded
high-test smoke.

Neon collapses
to fluorescent red-shift.
All-too-obvious gesture
of a dead-end trend.

The fugitive speaks:
"J'aime la ville ce, trou pisse ce."

Surrounded. Unquestioned.

III

We waited for some official vehicle, cops …
a clumsy scribble in the notebook.

Pencil-pinched between gloved fingers,
frozen vegetable-rot collage.

A wheeze mixes with
the white-noise-quiet of the city.

On a slender sidewalk
some guy a cough from death –

flotsam in the alley's mouth,
ice litter clotting the border.

Kensington Market proximate
a miscarried housing complex –

social democracy slows to sludge
in minus-twenty wind-chill.

"A stupid god made the world."
No, that won't work …

IV

A linear desert –
eight lanes spliced by an empty boulevard
cluttered with bypassed monuments.

The whole soft quiet of the night.

A low concrete bench.
A payphone outcrop to the east.

I could call her for space –
a futon layered with the gesso
of some other's output.

Slap down a paragraph about necessity.

V

44 Dovercourt late –
boozecan with Boîte à Chansons pretensions.
Salvaged candles sputtering
in too-good-to-be-true Chianti bottles.

In a taxi, kissing smudged lip-gloss,
Vodka-tang bellowing
from an art history mouth.

Coffee at noon without a name
to hang a promise on.

VI

... and on Queen Street West they wrestled,
raised storefront from its purpose,
re-purposed the Anglo rue's
ruins of commerce – 1981 Fodors says
it's army surplus, bargain junk –
say Simcoe to Cameron,
Soho recycled (Sandy Stagg,
her coterie valorized, gallerized).

[Rise up] all-sorts tramp north to Fiesta –
special of the era,
Pernod for the price of a beer.

... dots, artists, vomit-shadow, mechanical
extrusions
framing a General Idea –
fixed in motion.
Ancient video of a woman walking
through a conceptual gouge
in Grange Park –
the gifts return,
flatulent faltering bourgeois victories.

VII

There was something
I wanted to sing to you,
some necessary

throng of symbols.
A thousand relentless crickets,
thirty-thousand shrill starlings.

Like the incessant
half-remembered
nursery rhyme,

but the wind
swallowed voices,
songbird and raconteur.

You stayed ... sleeping
behind the duct-taped
brown-paper curtain.

I composed excuses,
thinking of form.
Avoiding police action.

VIII

... the young in each other's laps, lit up
with fifty-cent drafts.
A glass orchestra, contrapuntal coughs
up in the lofts of the bright, eyes in
woozy, tawny-beer colours, boxed
in the Beverly (haven) Tavern, room
at the inn for promiscuous punks,
puke-speckled theory, blood in the urinal,
piss-Christ, white powder
in a shit-brindle Datsun, huddled
with a leather jacket in the lee
of Peter Pan,
a few blocks from Paradise:

... ancient railway porters,
theoreticians,
a busybody busboy bumbling by
with words & foam-crusted half-pints –
a slim history of punishment.

... let me flirt in stardust,
be the gobbling up,
this crumbling I –
OK, yes you and thou,
let's sweep up roses.

IX

You wanted to tell me something about the way
you experience pain.

I wanted to explain very carefully
why the end of the world could never come too soon.

You said, "Let's build a stronghold with white linen
    napkins."
(Arranged in florets beside crystal glasses
buttressed by the crisp stucco walls
inside a realm of clean design.)

We'll be safe as projections in the gallery,
waiting for the siege to resume.

But the house is already on fire.
People screaming in the smoke.

X

Always night at the Ritz.
Basement jukebox museum
fraught with catholic cool.

Motown 45s – bomb shelter
regulars shun the stranger,
feign imperious, drowsy glances

under the sharp rule of fortified hip
bannered in neon-pink,
baptized with cigarette smoke.

An old man – probably 30 – circles
lisping revisionist Innis,
spitting simulations of McLuhan.

A leather beast bears witness,
petitions me – as "My Girl" snaps
and pops – "When there's nothing to say …
                    Shut the Fuck Up"

XI

La Chute in the Horseshoe –
Camus' bartender has shipped over.
The Amsterdam monster splashes
afternoon Heineken, ninety cents
a confession, "I flew over prairie
wasteland to join a reserve army
of post-punk poseurs."

The boy freshly bucked from Don Jail,
spills his shot of Jack, a Modernist
antique dealer argues the Virgin
Birth, the litigator licks
coke dust from his fingertips.

A mix-tape wobbles. The Clash blurts
"I Fought the Law." Themes converge,
precise as an essay deadline …

XII

Missiles impacted somewhere in the prairie, in the steppes,
seconds northeast and thousands southwest …

It was not the world or its simulation –
Twilight Zone
Just a sign in the stairway –
Voodoo Club
A call from the doorway –
Katrina's
A scrape in the alleyway –
Stages
Rules and functions in trim.

In from the wind to the sin of light,
the cleansing stench of poppers and sweat.
Gender-melting in flirting flame-licks.
Boys and girls and boys on the cusp
of any easy ecstasy any could slam
from sweet brain-cell dust,
the jolt of blood from heart
to homologous flesh stem.

I Just Can't Get Enough
In 20 minutes it could all be over.
Chant. Dance. Whoop.

The shape of my thought conforms to her skin,
Her prayers fellating me in the men's room,
"We are what we're permitted to sing,"
she says, swabbing her lips with my arm.

(We don't need this) Fascist Groove Thang
In 20 minutes it could all be over.
Chant. Dance. Warble.

It would not be the word or its imitation.
Just shortwave news in a scratchy idiom
delivered after last call.

Radio Silence
In 20 minutes it could all be over.
Chant. Dance. Whisper.

Retreat to the Empire Diner
for a caffeine cleansing.
The girl next to me is drawing
Jesus on her place mat –
lipstick on paper
with cooking fat.

Multiple Independently Targetable Re-entry Vehicles,
submarines, pump-jet silent, slipping by Alert.

XIII

"Christ of the disco dying with a sacrament of cocaine
sanctified by the method of its extraction
and the solidarity of the farm hands.
Ensuring the white powder is not profane,
not like the tallest tower in Christendom,
lit up for the pleasure of our shadow world.
Even non-believers know who fucks them up
more than mom and dad.
The dead man who asks for nothing
but disciples,
like the plain lines
of the Police Station that say nothing
but strength."

XIV

Milord I am not responsible for the factum.
It came before me from an unseen hand.
My testimony is terminal collage.

My lawyer's billing by the blink. My girl
will lie about the phallus but not this soul,
We scan newsprint surfaces for courtly news.

The court officers jabber 'bout bathhouse raids,
peers cannot be counted on to detonate guilt.
In this panopticon I'm an all-too-easy mark.

What dear punishment would you speak of?
Black Label & pretzels lasted all year.
The verdict will submit to the cut-up method.

XV

At the Cameron House it was explained,
Handsome Ned was fast-tracking to legend.
Obviousness was not to be faulted.

Pranksters and installation artists position
the tables, elbow out the pious critics –
stoned with transistor precision.

Daytime prices for what the keg spills.
They'd say Manhattan with dedication.
Shed salty lysozymes at the death of punk.

She planned a punch-drunk putsch
under the sign *This Is Paradise.*
He was published in and out of *Impulse.*

Some were serious spectacle heart-fuck.
This would be NFB documentary:
in the can a dry-tongue brush-stroke.

XVI

In the early edition
the ledes chum on.

Soviet crumbling,
America's slippy mooring.

Falling stars fell safe.
Bunker grammar held.

Neon Yorkdale glowed.
Certain broadsheets crowed.

Parliament enforced an easy
end-rhyme for market actors.

In this particular ceremony
the ready-made will do –

A ripe tobacco phraseme
seasons a snotty text.

At the Vesta Lunch we retch –
spit up this worn-out new.

XVII

For unity of thought demands –
samizdat copied.

Things broke –
razor-wire fortune rolled.

1989 and the genius of the Carpathians
dead.

Addresses no longer in order –
winter came back cold.

It was expected the tutor's rules
would bend.

Weapons linger in our bones.
Boys and Girls read on alone.

XVIII

The wind blows radiation east –
some fantasy of Lorca in the house of an old lover,
envy of the dead … Comrade K was in error.

There is a rust light over Etobicoke,
streetlamps are in remission.
I have returned to a clean white room.

a resistance

He's not worthy of the telling,
slipping off the page.

Mouth open in the third act,
soundtrack in shreds.

Go to him as he is not,
the master layers arguments.

She was always going to eat flesh,
they were subject to until now,

a concerto of fusty details.
Faultless followers replicate.

Someone has been killed,
an operation between integers.

Interference in the gods.
Scalpers misrepresent face value.

We did it on statutory holy days,
secular cancers of forced joy.

He was not among the celebrants.
She had the wisdom of curls.

In the desert night came early.
Out of sight, she oiled his skin.

Gneiss pebbles bled,
tears were blamed for droughts,

none were measured sufficient.
The task could not be dramatized.

A cut between characters …
it was as they believed.

The look in her eye of having been
a snake as beautiful as language.

film theory or i miss the way you kiss

The magical power that is attributed to taboo is based on the capacity for arousing temptation …
– Sigmund Freud

We killed a lot of gutter,
took hectares of blank space,
chopped up the I and you.
There wasn't much between X and Y,
just a lucky line that waggled through
crisp points on a reasoned grid.

Like poison's cure,
a ready-made story arc –
as if garlands of rose petals
redecorated the script
devolving from a set of probable causes
to a lazy desire for order,

razor ribbon fencing a glade
where lutes play, the prince reclines,
IEDs pop, blood-splatter browns
the long grass.

She says: "The days tasted of almonds."
He says: "Like smoked trout on a salted cracker."

Jump-cut to credits writ in jerky white:
the gun   ma blonde
the car   mon chum

agnostic ritual

There are days the Lord evades witness –
a geological absence.

Years prior to comets, rosaries,
semi-conductors ... before I
could scribble your name on a damp bar napkin –
the sure index of prayer's affect,

as the world splits
Lamentation from *Fountain*,

on afternoons when abstraction
suffices – or nights a jealous
god writes bad cheques,
outsources to the lesser angels.

let x = this

You say it's not easy to spit up a sense of ...
but I'm not listening *this* time ...
thinking of fortune and the fact
that *this*
                    is recalcitrant.

The world is all that is the case.

Pause to look over fields of suspect type,
splash Viognier into Val St. Lambert crystal,
crush fresh fig pieces between molars,
let the Morbier melt
                    as its ash salts our velum,
recompose this world phrase by drowsy phrase.

Squalls of reference ruffle our fancy talk
as you use me for explanation,
                    or something Anglo-Saxon,
a coital detour into argument.

We seek the lees of speech
                    with curious tongue-tips.

Whereof one cannot speak one must pass over in silence.

Sweep up the leftover alphabets—
                    stains of consensual lust
betwixt adjacent consonants.
Frame this thing we improvised.

Put the flesh of your words
                    between my top and bottom lips –
let me eat the meal of your complaint.

Yes, you and I, more or less spawning
in a polluted stream.

cahiers du cinéma

Once more an epic quality spills
Côtes du Rhône blood-tannin
from the cupped energy field
holding light's frame and tone.
   Un Homme et Une Femme

The here of it wrong,
the near of it alarm,
or the 'she' always asking,
and her glance backward –
Jack Nicholson lost somewhere in Spain,
running from pan to close-up.
   The Passenger

As if floating on a black river,
the fabric of fiction sinking –
a projector in flames.
Eyes lapping the screen
as the child ruptures the mise-en-scène.
An auteur dissolves into social conditions.
   Je vous salue, Marie

A hero under the drama's strict rule,
longing for a free story.
Dust motes on the lens,
singe of a dark star
   Les Enfants du Paradis

all we want is to look at art

All we want
(ever wanted) was to be on that
mailing list, parties at which slim caterers
offer red, yellow, black caviar
spilling off the triangular crackers
while off on the bay
rainbow-striped sails dip and bob and
twist.
  – Ron Silliman

Make way for magic!
Make way for objective mysteries!
Make way for Love!
Make way for the real necessities!
  – Paul-Émile Borduas

… that late painting, when she was thinning oils
with gasoline –
  Wind in the Treetops (1936-39)
  Emily Carr –
but my 13-year-old hated (was bored)
by representation.
Let him see the skin
of black leather sofas
harvested and sewn into a teepee –
  Furniture Sculpture (2006)
  Brian Jungen –
busting up proportions – provoking white tall walls
with repurposed cowhide. Well then you (or I) had him.

Like an abstract trap (1145 Georgia Street West) –
the mid-century VAG, where I'd ranged from colourfield
to white soaked and pricked convexed
surfaces … scumbling data into plastic argument
a diligent refusal to abandon
modern

... my son scrambles from realism
with beat gusto, getting the thingness
as I stare still,
Interrogating starved light
... recall the Artscanada critic
singing of infinite regression –

> *Byzantine Lights no. 68-73* (1977)
> Ronald Bloore –

Plain funeral rites – blue corn chips adorn
the Pinot Gris-splashed tablecloth. A gallery
talking to itself ... we await the canapés, glimpse
credentials from tight text squares.

The boy and the father at a walk-up motel –

> *What is it Daddy?* (1994)
> Ken Lum –

frame a performance reproducing Pacific suburbs –
gaudy with greeny ceremony –
an intimate copy that won't speak.

   Or daddy in Italian royal blue
windowpane and me—repositioned to 1973—
listening to Mr. Nixon's japes
re someone's colour splosh on a wall.

Provenance of scandal – absent black – shorn
sofas, slaughtered cows, the factory
where the leather must have been processed,
the plant sucked for pigment,
oil used, canvas stretched ... my son running
from Carr's raven.
"The weird art's upstairs," ... Nikes ripped,
rearranged as Haida masks –

> *Prototypes for New Understanding* (1998-2005)
> Brian Jungen –

He digs where grandfather lapsed, where
I fell in.
   Sea Gull (1956)
   Paul-Émile Borduas –
swells, thickening oil tides, a sea of jet-white
gesture.

We go into a black box where the tape is looping
Voyager's re-tale –
   Once Upon a Time (2004)
   Steve McQueen –
Life on earth all *Here Come the 70s*, in tongues
re-filtered with impatience for a single strand.

The kid's easy in fast collage – where I let Borduas
work form into my eyes –
skulks a pace or two, jonesing for the next
construct that must
be understood as really cool.
Who among us wouldn't want to see
a semi –
   Trailer (2002)
   Geoffrey Farmer –
re-presented as distilled spectacle?

Cages flank the ascending escalator
each contains desiccated lion shit –
father and son posed
within a wild frame.

some words after a crossing

where the bed changes unpredictable as the sea
tossing you up into the arms of lovers
with what fears of drowning you have never mentioned
   – bp Nichol

Crossing shimmering postcard water. Georgia Straight.
A twist up the Sea-to-Sky highway. The lasting picture
mountain, water, decrepit pier. A few injured frames of
her and then me, liquid behind us. We didn't talk about
the sea again. Had three days of Vancouver arguments
to look forward to before the Fraser Canyon silenced the
banter of left vs. right.

And that guy in the bar. Well shit, I should be on my
fucking knees thanking god for the privilege of just
breathing and being close enough to hear him chop
up his past like he was making kindling. But the drive
is long, I gotta get in the car and make it through the
mountains. He'll buy the round I'll miss, close the joint.
Go to sleep in Kamloops, untroubled by questions of
form and reader response.

The road and its fine cut: stories, streams, coulees,
sections, and the swirl of dust from the combine pushing
the unpaved shoulder into clouds in the heavy heat. As
you pass it at 160 klicks, pushing to Prince Albert before
nightfall. Maimed accounts of discursive practices: Ask
the waitress the time zone we're in.

He's kind of saying the feel of capitalism fucked up the
romantics who longed for authenticity and just enough
for everyone. Though there would be excess for artists,
who need it as farmers need predictable weather.
Listening to the CBC, pushing red on the Yellowhead.

Three-quarters there, from Saskatoon to Winnipeg with her asleep and the semis bearing down. Off the blacktop curve, the night on fire with crop-burn flames. We'll be in Toronto soon and soon enough divorced. Lost from this surging 5-speed acceleration: place names we'll collect but not inhabit.

"He writes," a thought turned, rounding Marathon. A caution for whereas and why, the smoke gates, the epistemic scatter, the acrid sugar of the pulp mill, and what's left after? I want to raise up evidence: forensic bits marked, tabbed with theory, tagged and set out among a jumble that will be an official record. The stuff we sort and stamp by; a place I got out to piss, 10 kilometres past Wawa.

Time's waste: the stiff bed we bruised ourselves on in Banff; an architecture of want; matches from an Edmonton bistro; a menu archived from the Soo truck stop; the hitchhiker's condom wrapper; something she said that the wind swallowed; the angle of her jaw in the rear-view mirror.

If I could learn the road's blur-text as I learned my first wife's lower case kiss. Explain the way sense unfurls, colludes with duration. There was getting from and to – paved distance – white rain on the asphalt map, word by slate-wet word: ocean-memory, rock-scrap, lake-cut and the milk-loom of arrival – drinking in all that absence.

train 40 to ottawa

Miles Davis obvious, she sits
a faint wash of smile
as I wipe newspaper
fingerprints off the laptop,
insert *Sketches of Spain*
(the Canadian arranger
a small font-swirl in the cover art).

Trumpet and castanets in old stereo,
left-right in new headphones.
The clatter and sway of the rail
this way from tower to town –
through scrubby gaps of the once bush.
November spaces, sprawl's
serrated border – field, rock, great lake.
The iron-road an insurgent parallel.

She's a painted character
unread, a plain woman asleep.
Leather jacket, gray slacks.
On at Oshawa, off to Ottawa.
Pre-Cambrian rumble
tumble of ice. Let it be simple
science as the boy and then girl
tip syllables – tongue to language –
jazz on about an ice age.

The shield-edge blur past Kingston.
Houses with sun-sharp geometry.
She's awake at Brockville –
but I stay silent as theory.
Miles' percussive trumpet protects as
the train-chat swells to dull dialectic –
Rideau's old locks,

Smiths Falls vacant factories,
watertower erasure –
here now knowing the Nation's
Capital, a close distance.

dead end on the renfrew road

at noon the blue above turned
to a green blur of moving trees
the felled log rolled under me
and we began the afternoon's cruise
looking at ourselves in the forest.
　　—Fred Wah

Not scat in the hand nor seagull wings on lichen.
Little things did not jell into larger motifs or crack
like sharp concepts rifling from a cogent tongue.

There was none of the seminar in this ad hoc break.
The plantings unproved, the dwarf trees stayed
in their haphazard places mocking our thoughts

of landscape, middle ground, and certain styles
of brushstroke that improve a scene or tell
you or me that something had been made.

The worms died out on a granite outcrop.
A thermos emptied of jasmine and flasks drained.
Scotch-drop on a lip and less to say about nature.

A spent 30-ought-six in the mud at road's end.
A cigarette butt. Resource practices. Some tied
to a tree in '93, standing with the Nuu-chah-nulth

choking clear-cut tactics in the dank cedar tang ...
We kept the truck running as our talk turned
back on itself – salmon dying into a home stream –

the blunt gut loss of words at the Iron Workers Hall;
Melwood Cutlery sings of the drowned at Second
Narrows; haulers and loggers; texts that test hard

reductions; hikers and connoisseurs of available
wilderness; discursive trysts at the Kinsol Trestle –
what's crafted, tricked out – any decrepit green lyric.

"Consciousness," one of us could've said, grinding
a match into the track of the tire. Koksilah River
hiss mashed up with our free-form forensics,

shell casing, poetics, assured not a man nor
woman could answer, for the whole filched
from our everyday, as we loaded the pick-up,

the dusk trip back to Cowichan wine, Salt Spring
lamb, without an accounting of motive or means –
the osprey off-course under a dark nimbostratus,

an ideogenic silence at this limit of travel,
broken in translation from gravel to blacktop.
One of us noted the deer, as we slewed a slant turn.

directions & instructions

Tack through sumac.
Scuff glaucous surface.
Scrape ochre from your throat.

Slip past wet needles.
Sense water reading ground.
Urge cyan from your eyes.

Notes

Essay: The epigraph is from Genesis 1:6, King James Version.

When We Agreed: The Yellowhead Highway runs from the Pacific Ocean to southern Manitoba through the Rocky Mountains. Howard O'Hagen's novel *Tay John* (1939) is an askew inspiration for this poem.

Summer of Love: "Hey, hey, hey just got back from the USA" – playground rhyme (circa 1966-68). "Sunny Goodge Street," recorded by Tom Northcott (1967), composed by Donovan Leitch (1965). "Marijuana, LSD, Scientists make it. Teachers take it. Why can't we?" – playground rhyme (circa 1966-68). "Look at a Baby," The Collectors, composers Howard Vickberg & Bill Henderson (1967). Kerrisdale, Altamont, and the British Properties are neighbourhoods in Greater Vancouver, B.C.

August, Lake: Shawnigan Lake is located on southern Vancouver Island.

Free Translation: *Prince Valiant* is a comic strip created by Hal Foster in 1937; distributor, King Features Syndicate. The poem contains appropriations and direct lifts from "The Wanderer" from the modern English version posted at Anglo-Saxons.net.

Lacan at the Ovaltine: The epigraph is from *Le séminaire sur "La Lettre volée,"* Jacques Lacan, translated by Jeffrey Mehlman, "French Freud" in Yale French Studies 48, 1972.

Only Sea Foods was a restaurant in Vancouver's Downtown East Side operating from 1917-2009, its neon seahorse sign was installed in 1951 and hauled away in 2010.

Army & Navy is Vancouver discount store. The Town Pump was a nightclub in Vancouver in the 1980s and '90s.

Nights in the City of the Dead: The epigraphs are from: "Opponents, Audiences, Constituencies, and Community," Edward Said, *The Anti-Aesthetic: Essays on Postmodern Culture*, Hal Foster, editor (The New Press, 2002); *La Chute*, Albert Camus, (Gallimard Editions,1972); "New York City" *Ready*, The Demics (1979).

II: Osgoode Hall has been the home of the Law Society of Upper Canada since 1829 and is located in Toronto.

VI: Sandy Stagg was a key figure in the transformation of Toronto's Queen Street West in the late '70s and early '80s. She was an original partner in the still operating Peter Pan restaurant; and owned and operated Fiesta, a café of the New Wave era, near Yonge & Bloor. General Idea was one of Canada's most controversial and innovative art collectives, key provocateurs and promoters of what became the Queen Street West art scene.

"video of a woman walking" is a hybridized reference to Michael Snow's Walking Women series (1961-67).

VIII: The Beverly Tavern, 1967-2003. Storied bar. The poem references the photo artwork, Piss Christ, by Andres Serrano (1987).

X: "My Girl" (1964), Robinson and White, as sung by the Temptations. *Shut the Fuck Up (Parts I, II & III)*, General Idea, (1985).

XII: Twilight Zone, Katrina's, Stages, and the Voodoo Club were nightclubs and after-hours joints, in 1980s Toronto. The songs: "I Just Can't Get Enough" *Speak and Spell*, Depeche Mode (1981) written by Vince Clark; "Radio Silence," *The Golden Age of Wireless*, Thomas Dolby (1982); "(We don't need this) Fascist Groove Thang," *Penthouse and Pavement*, Heaven 17 (1981).

XV: "This is Paradise" was and remains stencilled on the walls of the Cameron House tavern in Toronto. *Impulse* was a respected and groundbreaking art and literary magazine

published and edited by Eldon Garnet from 1971-1990.
http://www.eldongarnet.com/impulse_71.75.asp.

XI: The Horseshoe Tavern, 1947 to the present day Toronto.

XVI: "Neon Yorkdale" is a reference to the now removed neon artwork at the Toronto's Yorkdale subway station. The Vesta Lunch is a 24-hour diner in Toronto.

XVII: "the genius of the Carpathians" AKA Nicolae Ceausescu, 1918-1989.

Film Theory or I Miss the Way You Kiss: The epigraph from Freud is from *Totem and Taboo* (1913), various subsequent editions.

Let X = this: Both "The world is all that is the case" and "Whereof one cannot speak one must pass over in silence" are propositions from *Tractatus Logico-Philosophicus*, Ludwig Wittgenstein (1922), various subsequent editions.

Agnostic Ritual: *Lamentation*, Giotto (1305-1306); *Fountain*, Marcel Duchamp (1917).

Cahiers du Cinéma: *Un Homme et Une Femme*, Claude Lelouch (1966); *The Passenger*, Michelangelo Antonioni (1975); *Je vous salue, Marie*, Jean-Luc Godard (1985); *Les Enfants du Paradis*, Marcel Carné (1945).

All We Want is to Look at Art: The epigraphs are from: "What [the flower sermon]," *What*, Ron Silliman, (The Figures Press, 1988) and *Refus Global*, Les Automatistes (including Paul-Émile Borduas) (1948). "VAG" denotes the Vancouver Art Gallery.

Some Words After a Crossing: The epigraph is from "love song 1," *Zygal*, bp nichol (Coach House Press, 1998).

Train 40 to Ottawa: *Sketches of Spain*, Miles Davis, Gil Evans (Columbia, 1960); Smiths Falls, Ontario, formerly "Canada's Chocolate Capital," home to Hershey, Canada 1965-2010.

Dead End on the Renfrew Road: The epigraph is from "Lardeau/Summer 1964," Fred Wah, *The Contemporary Canadian Poem Anthology Vol 4*. George Bowering, editor. (Coach House Press, 1983). Melwood Cutlery is a Canadian singer-songwriter. The author once heard Mr. Cutlery sing of the tragedy commemorated by Vancouver's Ironworkers Memorial Second Narrows Crossing. Readers are encouraged to check out www.melwoodcutlery.com.

The Nuu-chah-nulth (formerly referred to as the Nootka) are one of the indigenous people of the west coast of Vancouver Island. The place names in the poem are located in the broader Cowichan Valley region of Vancouver Island, B.C., with the exception of the Ironworkers Hall which is located in the City of Vancouver.

Acknowledgements

I apologize for all my writerly sins to and heap gaudy bales of praise upon my exemplary and long-suffering editor Elana Wolff. My ceaseless gratitude is offered to Michael Mirolla for his support and encouragement; and gracious thanks to Connie McParland and the whole team at Guernica Editions.

I have been encouraged by the astute observations, casual grace and occasional wild caprice of many people in the floating world of Toronto poetry and territories proximate. I am particularly grateful to Phlip Arima, Alan Briesmaster, Luciano Iacobelli, Jacob Scheier, Jim Johnstone, Karl Jirgens, James Dewar, Sue Reynolds, Hoa Nyguen, Alex Boyd, Jacob McArthur Mooney, Stephen Humphrey, Liz Howard and Shannon Maguire for giving me pages, rooms and stages upon and in which to fail better.

I would like to thank the kind and gracious editors for publishing earlier versions of these poems: "Cahiers du Cinéma" was first published in *Rampike Magazine*, and reprinted in *INTER! INTER Art Actuel*; earlier versions of "At the Edge of the Dig" and "Film Theory or I Miss the Way You Kiss" appeared in *Rampike*. Earlier versions of "East of There" and "Train 40 to Ottawa" were published in *Misunderstandings*.

The first version of "Nights in the City of the Dead" appeared in the eponymous chapbook edited by Alan Briesmaster (Aeolus House, 2006).

Earlier versions of "Proceed in an Orderly Fashion," "Free Translation," "Cahiers du Cinéma," "Train 40 to Ottawa," "Let x = this" and the second version of "Agnostic Ritual" appeared in the chapbook *Free Translation*, Jim Johnstone, editor (Cactus Press, 2009).

Earlier versions of "Cariboo Ghost Town," "August, Lake," "Clinton at 45 Below," "A Resistance," "Summer of Love [as "We Didn't Know"], and "At the edge of the dig" appeared in the chapbook *Instructions for Pen & Ink*, Jim Johnstone, editor (Cactus Press, 2010).

About the Author

Edward Nixon was born and grew up in British Columbia, primarily in Victoria. He spent some of his childhood in B.C.'s Cariboo region, Vancouver, and Kamloops, as well as Portland, Oregon. Since 1984 he has lived in Toronto and is the proud father of a 19-year-old son. Having stumbled inconclusively in the thorny woods of academe, Edward currently toils in the private sector as the founder and Managing Partner of EN Consulting Group, a boutique public outreach consultancy located at the Centre for Social Innovation in downtown Toronto. He has hosted and curated the monthly Toronto reading series Livewords since 2008, and programmed and hosted the Diamond Cherry Reading Series from 2006-2007. He is a frequent contributor to *Rampike* and the author four poetry chapbooks: *Nights in the City of the Dead* (Aeolus House 2006); *Arguments for Breath* (lyricalmyrical 2007); *Free Translation* (Cactus Press 2009), and *Instructions for Pen and Ink* (Cactus Press 2010). *The Fissures of Our Throats* is his first full collection.

Printed in June 2014
by Gauvin Press,
Gatineau, Québec